Kindness to Share from A to Z

Written by Todd & Peggy Snow
Illustrated by Kirsten Sevig

SCHOLASTIC INC.

To Mom, the kindest person we know.
Love, T.S. and P.S.
• • •
To Alena, Aidan, and Mara for being so kind to me.
K.S.

ISBN 978-1-338-24485-4

Text copyright © 2008 by Todd and Peggy Snow.
Illustrations copyright © 2008 by Kirsten Sevig. All rights reserved.
Published by Scholastic Inc., 557 Broadway, New York, NY 10012,
by arrangement with Maren Green Publishing, Inc.
SCHOLASTIC and associated logos are trademarks
and/or registered trademarks of Scholastic Inc.

20   22

Printed in the U.S.A.   40

First Scholastic printing, October 2017

Edited by Pamela Espeland
Text set in Adobe Garamond Pro and Futura
Illustrations created using a crow quill pen, India ink, and watercolor on Fabriano paper

Kindness is for sharing
in what you say and do.
Being kind is good for others
and how you should be treated, too.

Ask someone to play with you.

Bring flowers to a person who needs cheering up.

Collect canned food for people who are hungry.

Do something nice for another person just because.

Entertain the younger kids at a family party.

Forgive someone
who makes a mistake.

Give someone a compliment.

Help clean up after dinner.

Invite the new kid at school to sit with you at lunch.

Join a good cause.

Kiss your parents goodnight.

Listen when others are talking.

Make cookies to welcome new neighbors.

Notice when someone is kind to you. Say "Thank you."

Offer to help without waiting to be asked.

Pick up after yourself.

Quiet down when others are trying to sleep.

Read a story to a younger child.

Say
"I love you."

Think before you speak.
Choose kind words.

Use other people's things with care.
Ask first.

Visit people in a retirement home.

Wait your turn.

eXplain how to play a game so others can join in.

Yell good things at a game, like "Yay!" and "Go team go!"

Zip a younger child's jacket.